a b i d e

BRAVERY FOR THE NEXT STEP

...for God gave us a spirit not of fear
but of power and love and self-control.

– 2 Timothy 1:7

ISBN 978-1-7360844-7-2

Published by Copperlight Wood
P.O. Box 870697
Wasilla, AK
99687

www.copperlightwood.com

Design by Shannon Guerra. Photography by Shannon Guerra, with the exception of pages 27-28 by Renee Petty and pages 57 and 59 by Megan Ancheta.

Portions of scripture in **bold** are the author's emphasis.

This title may be purchased in bulk for ministry or group study use. For more information, please email shop@copperlightwood.com.

Printed and bound in the USA.

contributors

MĒGAN ANCHETA
Kodiak kid, fearless knitter,
owner of Allergy Free Alaska, LLC
www.allergyfreealaska.com
allergyfreealaska@gmail.com

JESSICA DASSOW
lover of old-fashioned flowers, chicken collector,
seeker of sand & sunshine
www.planted-by-the-river.com

CYNTHIA HELLMAN
unsweetened sun tea drinker, over-analyzer
with a penchant for old canning jars
www.cultivatedgraftings.blogspot.com

RENEE PETTY
barefoot hiker, lover of flowers, greenhouse
gardener, dances in the kitchen
and laughs at her own jokes

PATTY SCOTT
heart encourager, road tripper, hip-hop
dancer, and author of *Slow Down, Mama*
and clean romance novels
www.pattyhscott.com

contents

grace to it

Do something that scares you every day.
Like, share queso with a toddler.
#hedoubledips #andnowIamwearingqueso

Or, like obeying God in something you feel completely unqualified for. Maybe that's the same thing.

Fortunately, God is deeply unimpressed with what we think we are unqualified for. He is deeply impressed and in love with surrendered hearts that obey Him anyway.

> *Then he said to me, "This is the word of the Lord to Zerubbabel: Not by might, nor by power, but by my Spirit, says the Lord of hosts. Who are you, O great mountain? Before Zerubbabel you shall become a plain. And he shall bring forward the top stone amid shouts of 'Grace, grace to it!'"*
> – Zechariah 4:6-7

I can think of a few mountains in my life that need more of the Spirit and less of my own might and power. I write books and teach kids and pray for people, and each of those things often leave me feeling promoted to a new level of my own ineptitude. God is constantly pushing me out of my comfort zone and showing me how much I need Him. Which, all things considered, is not a bad place to be. But it's almost never easy.

7

This guy Zerubbabel was a leader, a man of God, a craftsman assigned to the huge task of rebuilding the house of the Lord. He had to set boundaries with conniving, dishonest men, and when he did so he faced opposition and accusation. A quick search of his name throughout the Bible leads you to statements like these:

> Yet now **be strong**, O Zerubbabel, declares the Lord....**Work, for I am with you**, declares the Lord of hosts, according to the covenant that I made with you when you came out of Egypt. **My Spirit remains in your midst. Fear not.**
> - Haggai 2:4a, 5

So far, that sounds pretty good: *Be strong. Work. My Spirit is with you, fear not.* Great pep talk, I like it.

But there's also this:

> Speak to Zerubbabel, governor of Judah, saying, I am about to shake the heavens and the earth, and to overthrow the throne of kingdoms. I am about to destroy the strength of the kingdoms of the nations, and overthrow the chariots and their riders. And the horses and their riders shall go down, every one by the sword of his brother. **On that day**, declares the Lord of hosts, **I will take you, O Zerubbabel my servant**, the son of Shealtiel, declares the Lord, **and make you like a signet ring, for I have chosen you**, declares the Lord of hosts.
> - Haggai 2:21-23

And that sounds a little more ominous; God is warning Zerubbabel about the days ahead, when institutions we tend to depend on will be overthrown. He trusts him with that information, *and then tells him He has chosen him as a signet ring* – a symbol of authority and power. Signet rings were used by kings like a signature on a decree, declaring it authentic and in force. This man who did the work he was called to represented God's word in action.

Could it be that when we walk in what God has called us to, we are also representing God's word in action? It's much more serious than simply pressing toward a dream or working toward some ambitious goal. We trust God to use us because of His ability, not our own, and when we do that we represent the Kingdom's authority and power. When temporal authorities are shaken and the familiar systems we rely on are no longer dependable, our lives point to the final authority who we can always trust.

But we're not done yet, because there's also this:

> **The hands of Zerubbabel have laid the foundation of this house; his hands shall also complete it.** Then you will know that the Lord of hosts has sent me to you. For whoever has despised the day of small things shall rejoice, and shall **see the plumb line in the hand of Zerubbabel.**
> - Zechariah 4:9-10

In spite of attack and opposition, Zerubbabel finished the job God called him to. He was stalled for a while, but at the end of it, he held the plumb line – the tool that revealed the job had been accurately performed.

Those big hurdles, those towering projects, those callings that are so much bigger than we are? Our lives are yelling, "Grace! Grace to it!" as we obey in steadfast, holy stubbornness, and get the job done.

We represent Him only when we trust in His ability through us rather than our ability without Him. My career and my motherhood have driven me to Him like nothing else, because I know how unqualified I am without His Spirit showing me how to do them.

So I'm just over here at my desk, winging it at my computer and abiding hard with Jesus...while the toddler discovers the fridge's automatic water dispenser. Let the party begin.

telling our feelings
where to go

You probably know that to get specific results, you should pray for specific requests. So at the beginning of one year when we were praying and fasting for some major breakthroughs, we did that...sort of. What I mean is, we *specifically* prayed for everything. There was so much that we wrote a list. And we saw some gains right away in a few areas. Not perfect victory, but definite progress.

And finally, a couple months later, one issue completely resolved. We watched it with a little skepticism to see if it was for real – was it just temporary, or would it stick? – and it did stick. All better, *finis*. The relief was immense. I felt it physically, even: lifted, and lighter.

That feeling, Love? God asked. *You need to hold onto that feeling for all of those other concerns, every detail of them. I want you to picture what it would feel like for those concerns to be resolved, and feel it physically – feel the weight come right off. That is hope becoming tangible, and it is a powerful thing that allows the actual event to manifest.*

But I'll be open-heart honest here. I had felt so defeated in some of those areas that I'd forgotten how to picture the victory for them. (You could file them under "things we still pray for but don't want to talk about"). As a result, I hadn't felt the relief that comes with breakthrough for a long time. But I needed to start doing it again, because some of the other things on that list were a mess and completely out of my hands.

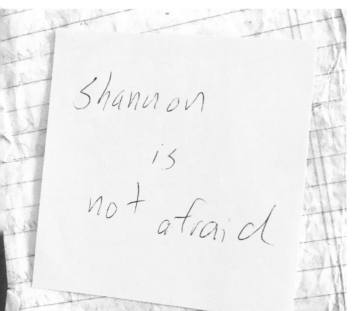

Vin gave me this note during that season of unknowing. It didn't feel true, but it was true in the sense that he was calling bravery out of me when I was feeling much the opposite. It was true as faith is true, when we believe and know truth in spite of what we see and feel, because what we see and feel can be manipulative and deceitful.

Our feelings are fickle, fleeting, and subject to being blown any which way. This is why the enemy uses them to manipulate us – especially right before a victory, when he feels threatened the most.

Not all thoughts are yours; some of them are directly from the enemy. If he can throw feelings (fear, doubt, discouragement, intimidation, to name a few) on you, it's an easy trick he will play over and over until you think prayer is useless and you give up on it, or you just go through the motions in a religious sort of way, checking off the box without gaining any victory.

Let's not fall for it, though.

> *In the fourteenth year of King Hezekiah, Sennacherib king of Assyria came up against all the fortified cities of Judah and took them. And the king of Assyria sent the Rabshakeh...with a great army.*
> *- Isaiah 36:1-2a*

Here's a quick history lesson, one sentence long: **King Hezekiah was in the middle of restoring Israel.** On the list of good kings and bad kings, Hezekiah was a good guy. Then an enemy king sent this punk Rabshakeh to him and his people to incite all kinds of bad feelings in them.

> *And the Rabshakeh said to them, "Say to Hezekiah, 'Thus says the great king, the king of Assyria:* **On what do you rest this trust of yours?** *....But if you say to me, "We trust in the Lord our God," is it not he whose high places and altars Hezekiah has removed, saying to Judah and to Jerusalem, "You shall worship before this altar"?.... Moreover, is it without the Lord that I have come up against this land to destroy it? The Lord said to me, "Go up against this land and destroy it." ' "*
> *- Isaiah 36:4, 7, and 10*

As usual, the accuser was using half-truths, lies, and false information. The enemy will do whatever it takes to keep us from God, and some of his main targets are our communication with God and our trust in God. This particular accuser repeatedly told the people to not listen to their king: *Do not let Hezekiah deceive you, for he will not be able to deliver you. Do not let Hezekiah make you trust in the Lord by saying, "The Lord will surely deliver us. This city will not be given into the hand of the king of Assyria." Do not listen to Hezekiah.*[1]

Then he told the people to make peace with *him*, the enemy threatening them. The hiss of the snake was strong with that one.

But you and me? We hear the same thing. Sometimes we feel like we can't hear God, or we don't know what to say to God, or we feel like God doesn't hear us. Usually though, we're paying too much attention to our feelings. Because our feelings are important but they are not an accurate gauge of reality.

So, some facts over feelings:

✛ God hears everything we say. He doesn't ignore us and He's never too busy to listen.

✛ We don't have to sound polished or perfect. We don't even have to say certain words. We just need to show up.

✛ God is not an intruder who invades, breaking and entering into our lives. He wants partnership with us, and requests permission to gain it. We have free will. He wants full access to your life but He will not help Himself to what you withhold.

✛ We gain nothing by withholding. We lose big time when we grasp at our pride and insecurities, refusing to show up in prayer and surrender. But good news, the opposite is also true — we gain more than we know or can imagine by partnering with Him in prayer, every single time. Every prayer equals huge impact.

✛ Every Christian is called to prayer. It's not something that's "just not my thing" or that only certain people are gifted in. We are told to pray — without ceasing.[2] It's not a suggestion or just a good idea.

So just start right now. One thought, directed at Him, is a good start. It's nothing fancier or more complicated than that.

We are in the middle of restoration and on the brink of promise, and the enemy spits doubts and accusations at us, promising a measure of peace if we'll only cower in fear. But we can never make peace with the accuser. There is no compromise that will ever make fear be quiet. All it will do is feed the beast, making him bolder and more obnoxious.

So, what happened to Hezekiah?

> Isaiah said to them, "Say to your master (King Hezekiah), 'Thus says the Lord: **Do not be afraid because of the words that you have heard**...Behold, I will put a spirit in [the enemy], so that he shall hear a rumor and return to his own land, and I will make him fall by the sword in his own land.'"
> - Isaiah 37:6-7

The enemy who tried to start rumors among God's people for their destruction fell prey to the same thing himself. It was his undoing.

Maybe you're like me. We know what's been promised, but the enemy still tries to harass us with doubt and hopelessness because he fears our victory more than we fear our failure.

But now we know better.

> *Now Faith, in the sense which I am here using the word, is the art of holding on to things your reason has once accepted, in spite of your changing moods. For moods will change, whatever view your reason takes....That is why Faith is such a necessary virtue: unless you teach your moods "where they get off," you can never be either a sound Christian or even a sound atheist, but just a creature dithering to and fro, with its beliefs really dependent on the weather and the state of its digestion. Consequently one must train the habit of Faith.*
> – C.S. Lewis [3]

We must ask God to be our filter, to protect us from lies and discouragement and propaganda. Then we can command a sense of relief and walk in peace, trusting God for the outcome He's promised. We won't let ourselves get this close to breakthrough only to lack the strength to walk in it.

falling forward

BY CYNTHIA HELLMAN

Someone once told me walking is falling forward and catching yourself each time.

As the mother of five daughters this is something I've seen demonstrated countless times. I've clapped and cheered as chubby legs took hesitant steps, all the while chuckling over their Wobbly Bottom Syndrome. Each step felt precious to behold. Then they began using this newfound skill to destroy everything in their three-foot high zone of terror...but I digress...

We all know the drill. Strong arms support those jelly legs until they can support themselves. Strong arms hug those same toddlers when they tumble. We capture it on video and in photographs.

I no longer have dimpled fingers holding onto my thumbs for stability; now I'm watching my oldest walk like a pro. I'm watching her walk right out the front door with the car keys swinging from her non-chubby, non-dimply, adult-like hands.

It still takes strength to encourage her to walk, to take the next step with Jesus, to march right into adulthood. It takes a different kind of strength to wave goodbye without journeying with her. What was once a *muscle thing* shifts more and more to a *soul thing*. But you knew that, didn't you? We mothers know we're working ourselves out of the job. And our mothers' generation nods their head in that bittersweet manner as if to say, "We know the feeling. Just look at *you*."

Sometimes I wonder what the next stage of life will look like. As the mother of many, it still feels a long ways away, but you and I know it'll be here in a blink or two. Where's the recipe in this volume? I need to go eat some feelings.

In the meantime, what a privilege to witness the brave next steps of countless individuals. Steps swirl all around us, and I'm not talking about health tracker gadgets counting our activity level. I'm talking about steps of faith, of desperation, of bewilderment. *How exactly did I arrive at this point, Lord?* I'm talking about the new mom who is exhausted by her badge of motherhood (and the dad who has no idea what to do about it). The person behind the devastating diagnosis, the crippling anxiety, the broken body who rises yet again. The moving van at the curb, the job transfer, the new school. I'm talking about the crumbling of the comfortable. Every day people I talk to are falling forward and catching themselves in the strong arms of an Everlasting Father.

Some next steps aren't as scary as others. Stepping across the threshold of something truly thrilling (and non-threatening) garners more confidence than stepping into a fuzzy "maybe." Those "maybes" are the toughest to lay bare before others for fear we heard wrong. *Lord, is this Your voice, my longings, an emotional pull, or just really bad heartburn?* Sometimes it seems as though His reassuring arms are too many steps away. The waves are too high, and the waters are too deep.

And Peter answered him, "Lord, if it is you, command me to come to you on the water."
- Matthew 14:28

Some next steps feel like white-knuckling the edge of the boat and sporting anchors for shoes. *Lord, do you really mean it?* Those are the toughest — we agonize over those steps, don't we, friends? It's tempting to freeze up, give up, or feign pious ignorance. I can't do this, so I'm not going to do anything of import. I can't do this, so I'm going to quit before I make a fool of myself. I can't do this, so I'm going to erect spiritual smoke and mirrors to falsely impress you with my shiny decoy.

God slices through our smoke and mirrors with His double-edged sword of truth and grace. It's terrifying to release our grip on the boat. The One who commands the currents knows your heart — He knows the fear and doubt that threaten a collapse of faith. He knows you feel a soul-deep bruising from the pummels of fear. Take heart; His pierced hands are waiting for you to trust Him for the next fall forward. Just take one step and fall into His waiting arms.

made for greatness

It doesn't matter how many toys we have, every two-year-old I've ever known loves finding the biggest pair of footwear available so they can clomp around the house in them.

We are made with this desire for greatness: to take on projects beyond our ability, to tackle impossible ventures, to commit exploits. To wear big shoes. Sometimes as adults we forget this, and we grow out of our bravery and make excuses for it, mislabeling fear as responsibility or prudence to make it sound better. But usually it's still just fear –a tired, jaded unwillingness to launch out of our comfort zone.

But let's not be that way. Not today, at least. Look at this with me:

> Now the Lord said to Abram, "Go from your country and your kindred and your father's house to the land that I will show you. And I will make of you a great nation, and I will bless you and make your name great, so that you will be a blessing.
> – Genesis 12:1-2

How many times has God told us to go and do something, promising His blessing along with it, but we've cowed and shrunk back? *Umm...nah, no thanks. That blessing sounds good, but I'm not sure it's worth it. Seems like a lot of work and unknowns, and too much risk. Thanks, but I think I'll pass.* For as many times as I have obeyed and moved out of the comfort zone, I've probably backed out at least twice as often.

But for those times I have obeyed, He's done more than I could've dreamed. He's brought the fire.

We tend to think that God won't do it for us, though. Fill in the blank, whatever it is: provide, heal, restore, transform, ease the burden, make a way. Help us fill those big shoes, and help us walk in them without falling over. He does it for others, though.

So we keep praying for Him to do it for others. We have faith that He will, for them. But not always for us. Why do we think we're the exception? Why do we think we're so special, so particularly undeserving?

Because we know us, and we diminish Him to our perception.

But He knows us, too, just like He knows them. And our differences aren't so huge that His blood didn't overcome them.

If you are feeling somehow less-than or undeserving, remember this: Twice in the Old Testament the Lord held water back so His people could move forward. He is still doing it over and over in our lives, if only we have eyes to see it. He is actively, lovingly making a way for you and for me, just like He does (and did) for them:

> For the Lord your God **dried up the waters of the Jordan** for you until you passed over, **as the Lord your God did to the Red Sea,** which he dried up for us until we passed over, **so that all the peoples of the earth may know that the hand of the Lord is mighty, that you may fear the Lord your God forever.**
> - Joshua 4:23-24

So that all the peoples of the earth may know: That's us. You and me and them.

That you may fear the Lord your God forever: Not fear your own circumstances or failures or inadequacies or excuses for why you are undeserving.

He is still taking the Jordan Rivers and the Red Seas in our lives and holding them back so we can walk forward. So we can write down words we've been putting off for too long. So we can look some ideas in the face and ask God what to do with them, and what He wants to do with us. So we can take those next steps in those big, unfamiliar shoes.

I can't imagine (and I don't want to imagine) what He would've done by now had I not been too afraid to do the other things I've backed down from. But I'm excited for what He's going to do from here on out.

Sometimes we look at our kids and their brilliant ideas, shake our heads, and smile, asking them, "What am I going to do with you?" And maybe God does the same thing with us, but He already knows the answer. So thank Him for knowing it. Ask Him for eyes to see it. And when He tells you to move in faith, don't hesitate. He has made us to achieve greatness, to walk in these big shoes, and people are watching for His faithfulness as we trust Him and do it.

"I should like to be a brave adventurer, like Mr. Oxenham."

"God grant you become a braver man than he! For, as I think, to be bold against the enemy is common to the brutes; but the prerogative of a man is to be bold against himself."

"How, sir?"

"To conquer our own fancies...and our own lusts, and our ambition, in the sacred name of duty; that it is to be truly brave, and truly strong; for he who cannot rule himself, how can he rule his crew or his fortunes?"

- Charles Kingsley [4]

the journey to high places

BY RENEE PETTY

We were about a third of the way up when I began to feel it – anxiety – niggling at the corners of my mind, growing increasingly more obnoxious with each step. Once an old friend, I had long since cut ties with it, refusing to allow it to determine the course of my life anymore. But here it was, on a mountainside, washing over me in waves, tempting me back to my old comfort.

Left foot, right foot, left foot – *what do I do?* Right foot, left foot, right foot – *do I turn around?* Left foot, right foot, left foot – *am I going to ruin this for everyone else?* Turn back, hold still, press forward – right foot, left foot...you get it.

It's the age-old internal battle – am I going to move forward when faced with adversity? Am I going to freeze here, hoping it passes? Am I going to retreat back to my safe space, regardless of how unsafe it truly is? For many years I rarely ventured outside my comfort zone, let alone pressed forward. Fear and anxiety hemmed me in so completely that at its crescendo I was terrified to leave my house, and I thought there was no way ahead.

Grit, spit, and duct tape, it's the American way. When we need to move on in life, we pull ourselves up by the bootstraps and take that next step – but that kind of living becomes an exhausting battle of will, and Jesus has a better way. Prayer, worship, and surrender are the tools He's given us when we're called forward but we're tempted to retreat. A life abiding in His presence, a will surrendered to Him – and He supplies all we need.

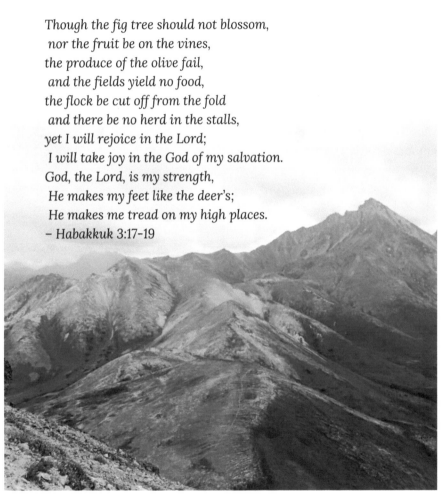

Though the fig tree should not blossom,
 nor the fruit be on the vines,
the produce of the olive fail,
 and the fields yield no food,
the flock be cut off from the fold
 and there be no herd in the stalls,
yet I will rejoice in the Lord;
 I will take joy in the God of my salvation.
God, the Lord, is my strength,
 He makes my feet like the deer's;
 He makes me tread on my high places.
– Habakkuk 3:17-19

The Lord is my strength – He makes me tread on my high places. Simple, and yet not so, but He is faithful and will give us what we need when we cry out to Him. Left foot, right foot, left foot. Step by step He takes us up the mountains.

I am happy to share that I made it to the top of that not-so Lazy Mountain that day, and have made it to the tops of other, less literal mountains in the days since. Each journey is an opportunity to know Him more, to grow in both trust and surrender. I have discovered that I am capable of much more than I ever thought when He is my strength. With feet like a deer, we scale the highest places together, and I have seen more beauty and experienced more joy and more freedom than I ever thought possible.

Where is the place Jesus is calling you to that you feel is an impossible height? What are the areas in your life that are surrendered to fear instead of to Him? Where are you striving to find the strength to move forward? *Though the fig tree should not blossom...yet I will rejoice in the Lord...the Lord, is my strength.* Let Him be your strength. He will be faithful, and together you can take that next step.

when our favor looks like fear

The sky was getting dark. There was tea and dimmed lights and the glow of the computer screen, and a book sitting at my left elbow.

It was my book, the first little one I wrote. We'd spent a year (and a stupidly ridiculous amount of money) reworking it. We had invested hours in phone calls and paperwork and, oh yes, angsting over the cover, which was the whole reason I wanted to relaunch it in the first place. We prayed, and God was clear: Relaunch that baby. Pay the money, let someone else do the work. Easy.

Ha. God is such a troublemaker sometimes. That stupid-easy cover was the hardest part of the process, and it turned out it wasn't why He had us relaunch anyway. Sometimes we think we know what we're doing; He humors us in our childish confidence, and then makes us wiser when we're ready for it – which is usually after we're already committed.

The reason He had us relaunch it had a lot to do with the paperwork I spent days praying over and filling out. Here are some of the questions:

What languages do you speak fluently? English, heavily dosed with sarcasm.

Is your name ever mispronounced? What is the correct pronunciation? Yep. Guerra sounds like "Gara," rhymes with "Sara" (so if you've ever wondered, now you know).

How would you like to be addressed? Just my name, thanks – no bowing or saluting, please.

But there were also some hard, scary questions: *Are there any relevant facts you would like us to use in your press material? Is there any "back story" that inspired you to write this book? What is the most controversial aspect of your message? If asked, are you willing to travel for an interview? If so, how far?*

And then, this whopper:

Are you comfortable talking about your book in public?

And friends, I LIED.
I said yes.

 Shannon Thornsley Guerra
23 hrs ·

That moment when you have to study your own book because it feels like you are taking a test on it from your publicist. #whatismybookabout #ihavenoidea
#tellusaboutyourself #howaboutno
#Whatwouldyouliketotalkabout #istalkingreallythatnecessary
#introvertproblems #prayforme

God had been so clear to us about this next step. There was no confusion, it was as if He handed us a map. But was I comfortable? No. Way, way, no.

But if He asked, was I willing?

This was why He let me believe we were just redoing the book cover. And I think this is why He often waits until we're committed to tell us what's really ahead. Sometimes a little ignorance helps us obey.

I had been reading about this happening a lot to someone else, too. It's back in the beginning, though, so come walk with me a bit:

> *Then the Lord said to Jacob, "Return to the land of your fathers and to your kindred, and I will be with you."*
> *- Genesis 31:3*

This is Jacob, son of Isaac, grandson of Abraham. God told him what to do and where to go. Easy. And we keep reading:

Jacob went on his way, and the angels of God met him. And when Jacob saw them he said, "This is God's camp!" So he called the name of that place Mahanaim. And Jacob sent messengers before him...
  - Genesis 32:1-2a

Mahanaim means "two camps." Why was Jacob prompted to call it that? Did he mean his camp and God's camp? Did he mean something else?

We keep reading:

And the messengers returned to Jacob, saying, "We came to your brother Esau, and he is coming to meet you, and there are four hundred men with him." Then Jacob was greatly afraid and distressed. He divided the people who were with him, and the flocks and herds and camels, into two camps, thinking, "If Esau comes to the one camp and attacks it, then the camp that is left will escape."
  – Genesis 32:6-8

Jacob had good reason to be afraid. This Esau, his brother, had threatened to kill him years earlier. God's prompting to name that place "Mahanaim" was His answer to Jacob ahead of time when Jacob had no idea what was ahead of him. God knew Jacob would need to think fast, so He put the answer at the ready before Jacob even knew he needed it.

He split his family, servants, and belongings into two camps. And then he prayed.

> And Jacob said, "O God of my father Abraham and God of my father Isaac, O Lord who said to me, 'Return to your country and to your kindred, that I may do you good,' I am not worthy of the least of all the deeds of steadfast love and all the faithfulness that you have shown to your servant, for with only my staff I crossed this Jordan, and now I have become two camps. Please deliver me from the hand of my brother, from the hand of Esau, for I fear him, that he may come and attack me, the mothers with the children. But you said, 'I will surely do you good, and make your offspring as the sand of the sea, which cannot be numbered for multitude.'"
> - Genesis 32:9-12

He knew the word from the Lord. He knew the direction he was going. Yet there was a threat in front of him and he was scared, so he also needed to remember what God had promised him. Because if God had given him a word that wasn't yet fulfilled, Jacob knew he would get where God was calling him in spite of the threat standing in the way.

Some of us have a word and direction from God in this season, too. And even in our obedience and following, we fight fear, doubt, insecurity, and a slew of evil hosts.

A dangerous brother was ahead, and then he wrestled a stranger[5] in the night. Like us, Jacob faced several threats at a time – the car breaks down, and then the heat goes out. Or there's a leak in the ceiling, and your husband has kidney stones. One thing after another. We wrestle with God in the darkness and night, asking Him our hard questions, exposing our anger and fear. *You told me to go this way, so why is this in the way? Why did you send me here only to face this threat?* We accuse Him of not caring, or playing a trick on us, and somehow lightning does not strike us.

Our honesty doesn't throw Him. It brings us right up to His face and He reminds us that we were the tricksters, the sinners, the ones who needed grace. He gives us the identity of favor. Brushing our old issues under the rug always hurts us; our honesty enables us to hear His truth, and we live. We survive the encounter and come out delivered.

Not only that, but it's possible that the hosts headed our way are actually on our side. The obstacle we fear might actually be the favor we were afraid to hope for.

> *But Esau ran to meet him and embraced him and fell on his neck and kissed him, and they wept.*
> *- Genesis 33:4*

Jacob tells his brother, *I have seen your face, which is like seeing the face of God, and you have accepted me* (Genesis 33:10). Jacob encountered both God and Esau. He didn't think he could survive facing either of them, much less receive favor and blessing from both of them.

Should I really pursue publicity? My little book about supporting adoptive families made no apologies for calling the media out. Much of adoption's misrepresentation and the subsequent lack of support to adoptive families can be laid squarely at the media's feet, and my book said so. Could I really expect favor and help from the same profession? I didn't want my voice to shake. I didn't want to misrepresent or give the wrong answers or say something scandalous. I wanted to be humble, but not humiliated.

But He said, *When I send you somewhere, Love, you don't go empty handed. You go with favor and authority. I won't send you anywhere that I'm not going Myself.*

The message He gave me was a lifeline for adoptive families. Months later when I spoke into a microphone, it wasn't just a breakthrough for me; it was a breakthrough for those families who

were on the brink of collapse, desperate for people to understand what they were going through. We were fighting the same enemy, and my obedience was a win for all of us.

> *Then let us arise and go up to Bethel, so that I may make there an altar to the God who answers me in the day of my distress and has been with me wherever I have gone.*
> *- Genesis 35:3*

What if the enemy was so afraid of your victory ahead that he tried to disguise it as a threat you would try to avoid?

How many victories have we rejected because we succumbed to the manipulation of fear?

If asked, are we willing?

He is speaking answers to us before we know we need them. The obstacle we fear might be the favor we're afraid to hope for. And the victory we step toward is never just for ourselves – generations ahead will be impacted by our brave obedience.

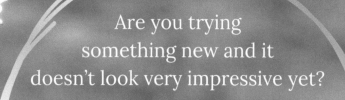

Are you trying
something new and it
doesn't look very impressive yet?

Well, perfect!

That's how growth works.

Good, beautiful, life giving
stuff starts here.

facing the future without fear

BY PATTY SCOTT

A group of us sat around the living room, some of us strangers, some long-time friends. All gathered to spend a night connecting just because I came to town. The conversation went deep within the first half hour as we talked about family, Jesus, and our hopes and dreams. And then we started talking about fears.

It wasn't your usual women's gathering, to be sure. When my turn to share came, my first instinct was to say, "I don't really have any fears." And I meant it. It's a lot like when someone asks me my most embarrassing moment and my response feels like it ought to be, "Right now, while I'm standing here on the spot, unable to come up with one embarrassing thing on the spur of the moment." I freeze and my usually quick mind can't muster up anything self-revelatory.

I thought I had no fears because I've overcome so many. I've walked through healing journeys and laid my fears at the foot of the cross. I've studied the verses where God repeatedly says, "Fear not," and "Be anxious in nothing." My trust has grown. Ironically it has grown most while I wandered away and then was drawn back, only to measure the distance of my wandering by His patience and love for me under all circumstances. I've learned how He stays, even when I stray—how He holds fast while I wrestle. And those times have taught me how deep the Father's love for me truly is.

And perfect love has cast out fear. [6]

As we went around the room that night, women shared fears. And one woman said, "I'm afraid of knives." Me too! Like, deathly afraid. I sliced myself as a teen and it left me with a fear that has always lurked beneath the surface. I get the willies around knives. It's like I fear they are going to jump up and slice me unbidden. It sounds ridiculous, just like most fears do in the face of reality.

When I opened the cork to acknowledge my one fear, more awareness came ... fear, after fear, after fear. Turns out, I'm still afraid.

It's because we have fear that Jesus tells us "Fear not." Why would He say it if we didn't need to hear it? If we weren't mired in fear, He could avoid the encouragement in the form of a command. He knows we fear. That's why He tells us to let it go and trust Him, over and over and over and over.

And one of the things we fear most is the future—the unknown, impending next thing. What if we fail? Or mess up? Or look ridiculous and get rejected? Those under-the-surface fears can keep us sitting still in the seemingly safe present where at least we know our surroundings and can cope. It's in the here and now that I maintain a false sense of control. But God is always doing a new thing.[7] He is always moving toward our growth and freedom. Just as stagnant water becomes toxic, a life not flowing toward Him and with Him becomes toxic and ineffective.

So, we need to recognize the fears that keep us paralyzed. We need to name them and face them. But we never face them alone. He knows where He's calling us, and He knows what's keeping us stuck. And when we know what He knows, we can work with Him in overcoming those barriers.

Sometimes we wonder which way to turn. We face a fork in the road, or a big decision. We fret over getting it right. That concern is riddled with unspoken fears as well. What if I mess this up? Will God abandon me when I pick the wrong thing, even though I thought I was doing His will?

Let's consider those thoughts in light of Scripture. God tells us that He is a Good Father and He reminds us that even if we, who are evil, have a child who asks us for bread, we wouldn't give him a stone.[8] Would you abandon your child if they made a wrong move while trying hard to obey you and discern what you wanted? Of course not. Neither will your Good Father.

Step out.

Risk.

Take that next opportunity.

He is Emmanuel—God with you. He knows how to course-correct and He won't waste a drop of what you go through as you take these next steps. Know your fears. Bring them to Him and to trusted friends. And then, remember you are loved so deeply and held so dearly that you will not fall or fail. Even if you go down what seems like a dead end, or you miss what appeared to be a golden opportunity, or you make a huge mistake, He is with you and He will work all things together for your good and His glory.[9] He really will.

the keeper

Jesus. Just saying His name is a good start when the wind is blowing something crazy, and it's not just the weather.

> *I lift my eyes to the hills —*
> *where does my help come from?*
> *My help comes from the Lord,*
> *the maker of heaven and earth.*
> — Psalm 121:1-2

He is the one Who has the first word and the last word. And that's good to know because the trees are swaying wild, and they've fallen and hit our house before. But most of the time, it's just wind — just loud, just gusting, just a reminder of how vulnerable we would be without these walls around us. How vulnerable we would be without His arms around us.

> *He will not let your foot be moved;*
> *he who keeps you will not slumber.*
> *Behold, he who keeps Israel*
> *will neither slumber nor sleep.*
> — Psalm 121:13-4

Our fears and stresses are like that, too. Sometimes we do have a close call, and sometimes they really do touch down and hit our house — but most of the time, it's just wind, reminding us that we are vulnerable and yet covered. And even when they hit our house, we are still covered, because He is the garrison around us.

> *The Lord is your keeper;*
> *the Lord is your shade on your right hand.*
> *The sun shall not strike you by day,*
> *nor the moon by night.*
> — *Psalm 121:5-6*

He keeps telling me, *Hey Love, stop spinning your wheels and move forward in prayer.*

Make progress by reading pages on paper, not screens. Ignore the bait on social media to challenge, argue, pontificate, and assume. Close the app and do something productive.

And then go to bed, and remember the rest of the Psalm:

> *The Lord will keep you from all evil;*
> *he will keep your life.*
> *The Lord will keep your going out and your coming in*
> *from this time forth and forevermore.*
> — *Psalm 121:7-8*

We can choose not to partner with fear. And then we can go to sleep and rest, because God is awake.

good for you

On the scale of healthy eating, our family falls pretty close to the middle. We've learned to make good-for-you things like bone broth, homemade yogurt, and all kinds of foods and sauces from scratch, but at the same time we've also learned to make artisan breads, chocolate, and candies. And not all of my healthy efforts have been a success – there was a terrible period when I traumatized everyone with using swiss chard in smoothies. In case you were wondering, "swiss chard" and "smoothies" should never, ever, be used in a sentence (or a blender) together.

But some of my efforts have been great successes. People seem to either love or hate kombucha, and my kids love it. I'm convinced that most of the people who hate it had the experience ruined by bad commercial stuff from the grocery store.

 So when skeptical friends come over, I tell them in my mom voice, IT'S GOOD FOR YOU. JUST TRY IT. (I admit it; I am a kombucha pusher.)

But the same is true of a lot of good-for-you things ruined by commercialism, image fakery, bad ingredients, and staleness. Like prayer...like church...like reading great classic books...like a lot of things.

When we have a hard time with these good-for-you things, we often struggle with it. *I know these are good, important things, so am I not good for not liking them?* The Holy Spirit meets us in this struggle as we abide, honest-to-God with our feelings, wounds, and mistakes – our mistakes, and the mistakes of others.

Listen, friend: Your worth isn't changed by your choices.

Did you hear that? Your value is not diminished by your mistakes. Not the mistakes of others, either. It's not adjusted based on your circumstances or how people treat you or whether you've got things all figured out or not.

He restores, redeems, and refines us in our encounters with Him, when we need answers and we're brought face to face with our need for His light. It took me a long time to realize that this is why He made me a writer, because I wrestle with Him on the blank page and that is where I hear Him most. He always brings color and form to my chaos.

Are you in a different place than you thought you would be a week ago, or a year ago? It's okay. Hold these days with an open hand and let the Lord redirect them. It's not failure. It's growth.

43

We are all learning and growing. That's a healthy part of life. What is *not* healthy is to refuse to learn and grow, or to stagnate in shame, wallowing in the enemy's lies about worthlessness. The time to turn around from that is this very second.

When the enemy comes at you with those lies, remind him that YOU KNOW HE'S A LIAR (yes, use your mom voice) and then start talking to God about the truth. Ignore the enemy and focus on God's presence. Tell Him the things you know are true (and, remember: your feelings don't define what is true). Tell Him you know you are loved, you know He saw such value in your life that you were worth His life on the cross. Thank Him for your car, your house, your family, your bed. Tell Him that you know He is good and loving and true and taking care of you.

This is both worship and prayer. It changes you, helps you sleep better, helps you have happier dreams, helps you wake up in more peace tomorrow. And the enemy can't stand to be around it. It's the best way to end a hard day.

Our ministry is birthed out of what we overcome. Let's not give up on the good-for-you things just because we had a bad experience. Be brave and try again. Even with swiss chard (just not in smoothies).

Your victory is not just for you, but for your community, your kids, and the Kingdom. So keep fighting for that breakthrough, and steward it well.

So this has been me in my mom voice, preaching to all of us, including me. Glad we had this little chat.

lessons from my garden

BY JESSICA DASSOW

On a glorious day, I press seeds gently into warm soil. Many consider this the best part of the gardening year, but it's nerve wracking for me. Does that seem strange? I adore the planning, especially in midwinter when a white blanket covers my garden space and I sit with hot tea, poring over seed catalogs. Pen in hand, I sketch out dreams and possibilities, neatly labeling each section with the type and variety of plant I hope to sow.

When the snow melts, I enjoy readying the soil to receive its seed: amending with compost and adding mulch. It's during this time of year that I look through and study beautiful seed packets with anticipation, and I need to stay disciplined to not plant too early. Finally the weather warms and it's time to plant! It's exciting, until it's not, and that is where I find myself on this particular day.

As I sow each seed and cover it up, I can no longer see what's going on. I don't know if they will actually sprout. I'll need to be vigilant with watering; it's so easy to forget. I don't know if the

45

water will wash the seeds out of place. The rows may or may not be straight, and this won't be revealed until seedlings emerge. *Will they emerge?* Maybe the seeds are bad. Inevitably the cat is going to get (ahem) confused over the purpose of these giant, dirt-filled boxes. What if she digs out my seeds just as they germinate and I have to do this all over again? It's messy business with so many unknowns. My mind reels, and I suddenly realize it's because the questions aren't just about the plants I'm trying to grow.

You see, I also tend to the growth of five sons and a daughter. They're growing in different, sometimes unpredictable ways and at different rates. From each of their beginnings, I've held them tenderly, lightly, with anticipation, like beautiful seed packets brimming with possibilities. Currently they're all in different phases of growth – being planted, germinating, taking root. I have two sons in the process of bursting forth into wild growth and pursuit of purpose. It's unsettling that I can't always see what's going on, and yet that is the way with motherhood.

I hear man-laughter, and I look across the yard to see my sons helping their dad spread gravel on the driveway. Deep voices banter, smiles flash, muscles bulge, and I am keenly aware that all of them are home at. this. moment. I relish that knowledge, smiling bravely while tears sting

just a little at what will come to pass in a few short weeks. Our eldest will take off north to Alaska to commercial fish on an island in the Pacific. The second eldest, with high school gradua-tion behind him, will technically be home yet he won't be; he'll be wearing great big boots and climbing scaffolding. The third will head to a neighboring state for a work opportunity. The seeds will be planted, and I'll have to trust the Son to shine upon them and the watering to happen at crucial times. Just like that – our kid count will be halved, and we'll have a taste of what our next chapter holds.

I'm proud and I'm excited for these young men of ours. I'm also questioning if I taught them all they need to know, if I loved them enough and well, and if I loved them in ways they perceive as love. I'm wondering how they'll use what I've taught them, what choices they'll make, and what paths they'll take. The questions and what-ifs exhaust me and tie me up in knots if I let them. And though I'm tempted to convince myself that I didn't do enough and that disaster may lie around the corner, I take these questions to the One who gave us these precious souls to look after, invest in, and love. I ask Him, and I hear affirmation speaking to my heart. Yes, I've done enough. Because He is more than enough.

> *And I am sure of this, that he who began a good work in you will bring it to completion at the day of Jesus Christ.*
> – Philippians 1:6

I've tended to the soil and tucked those precious seeds into place. I've introduced them and led them to the One who saves. I've taught them right from wrong. I've trained and discipled. I've loved them fiercely. And here's the most important part – I've done this all so imperfectly, yet even so, it is enough. His grace covers all, and the good work He's begun in them will be brought to completion. He'll bring about transformation and miracles of sanctification within them. He will do all this, never slumbering or sleeping, without me seeing all the details He's working out beneath the surface.

And with this knowledge seeded deeply in my soul like so many seeds scattered and pressed carefully into the garden beds I'm tending, I continue on with my work. Catching sight of the bed I planted a few weeks ago, I admire beautiful, brave seedlings which have emerged, and mostly in straight rows. The Master Gardener has tended and cared for what I could not see, and He has brought order and beauty. This makes me smile as I think of my sons. They're ready for their next steps, and so am I.

It is not the critic who counts;
not the man who points out how the strong man stumbles,
or where the doer of deeds could have done them better.
The credit belongs to the man who is actually in the arena,
whose face is marred by dust and sweat and blood;
who strives valiantly;
who errs, who comes short again and again,
because there is no effort without error and shortcoming;
but who does actually strive to do the deeds;
who knows great enthusiasms, the great devotions;
who spends himself in a worthy cause;
who at the best knows in the end the triumph of high achievement,
and who at the worst, if he fails, at least fails while daring greatly,
so that his place shall never be with those cold and timid souls
who neither know victory nor defeat.

— Theodore Roosevelt[10]

in the upheaval

It happens here with every major change, whether it's from pregnancy, birth, extended illness, or any other upheaval: After several weeks (or months) of shaking up our normal routine, I completely forget how to cook.

I also forget what I like to cook, and that I actually enjoy cooking. It's months before I feel like I'm me again, doing the things I remember and love, and finally settle into the new groove.

One year brought more major shake-ups than normal: A move, a pregnancy, Vince quitting his job and starting to work with me from home, increased involvement in ministry. So many changes. A million loose ends needed to be addressed, but they were easily put off – like the dishes, ugh – because they weren't urgent. But things get harder and more cumbersome the longer they're put off, like oatmeal calcifying on breakfast bowls. There is no off switch for back burner tasks; they just keep scorching while left unattended.

I don't mean to give the impression that things here were in utter chaos. We got into some beautiful routines that we had prayed about for years – we read in quiet evenings, we got together with friends, we actually went to events and meetings we'd always had to miss before. All of the after-hours activity was in great form; it was the million cogs of the workday that was overwhelming, new, and still shaking out.

> *May the Lord answer you in the day of trouble!*
> *May the name of the God of Jacob protect you!*
> *- Psalm 20:1*

So much of getting it all done (whatever "it all" is) is the mindset of knowing I've already done something before and I can do it again, even if it looks a little different this time.

I have met this deadline before; I can meet it this month, too.

I've never had eight kids before, but I have had a baby before. I can do it again.

I've never figured out how to put page numbers on a document before, but with the help of the internet, I have figured out technical things before. So regardless of how much I hate doing it, I can push through and figure out how to do this, too.

> *May he grant you your heart's desire*
> *and fulfill all your plans!*
> *May we shout for joy over your salvation,*
> *and in the name of our God set up our banners!*
> *- Psalm 20:4-5a*

I could create a scaffold, and build off things I had already accomplished. Or, I could freeze in the overwhelm of being behind (and we exaggerate to ourselves how far behind we are, don't we?) and wonder if it was even worth the effort to try to catch up again.

We fall out of favor with ourselves when these tasks are still on our to-do list, just as we often think we fall out of favor with God when we sin – and instead of approaching the throne (or the desk) boldly, we shrink back in shame and defeat. [11]

We wear ourselves out feeling overwhelmed, ill-equipped, and unqualified for the day ahead before it even comes. And no matter who we are or what we do or why we're exhausted or what is ahead of us, at the end of the day we are all just one of God's little kids, overtired from playing too hard and staying up too late, and we need our Daddy to tuck us in and tell us it'll be okay and that everything will look brighter in the morning. He often tells us the same thing we tell our kids when they are overtired and all worked up: *Go to sleep.*

In that season when I was tired and whiny and fighting despair, I remembered to pray in reverse, thanking Him for all the things that were stressing me out: the sick cat, the specialist referral, the relationships and responsibilities. And then I opened the Word, and the bookmark was at Psalm 20, but I didn't recognize it was the same Psalm I'd read the day before. It was different this time because I needed it more.

> *May the Lord fulfill all your petitions!*
> *- Psalm 20:5b*

When I got to the end of verse 5, He asked me, *If I fulfilled all your petitions, would you be satisfied with what you asked for? Or would you feel like you'd left some things out and settled for less?*

Would you pray differently if you knew I was going to answer each one?

So I prayed more, laying them all out there, moving from the top tier of worries to the things I had deemed lower priorities, smaller fires that needed putting out, but in my attempts to urgently prioritize I'd left them out.

And this is another example of how His ways are not our ways because He is not frantic like we are. He sees it all on the same page and doesn't dismiss any of our concerns as unworthy.

> Humble yourselves, therefore, under the mighty hand of God so that at the proper time he may exalt you, casting all your anxieties on him, because he cares for you.
> - 1 Peter 5:6-7

They were things I had already prayed about, so I knew it was safe to stop asking Him and start thanking Him for answering, instead.

> Now I know that the Lord saves his anointed;
>   he will answer him from his holy heaven
>   with the saving might of his right hand.
> Some trust in chariots and some in horses,
>   but we trust in the name of the Lord our God.
> - Psalm 20:6-7

What is burdening you? The opposite of that is what God is up to. We feel overwhelmed with the tasks, but He is constantly accomplishing things and teaching us to be like Him. We chastise ourselves for being undisciplined, and He is constantly growing our abilities and capacity. **We would not feel overwhelmed and stretched if we weren't expanding**.

The more often we engage in an activity, the easier it is to stay in the groove of doing it. It takes a while, but we *do* get there and the hard things become easier things, the intimidating things become familiar things. As we abide, we develop new, good habits in the middle of changing schedules and responsibilities. Given enough time, they become almost self-propelling – wind in our sails, right in the middle of the upheaval.

farmbake

This is my favorite. I think I keep saying that, but I really mean it this time...probably. We started making it about twenty years ago when we found it in an old Irish cookbook, and have since renamed it (from "Irish garden vegetable bake" or something equally exciting) and modified it to our liking. It is our go-to comfort food: the best dish to take to a family who just had a baby, and perfect for potluck dinners.

This works just as well with white potatoes as it does with sweet potatoes, the bacon can be substituted with any number of things or eliminated entirely (but whyyy?!), and mushroom haters can use broccoli instead and follow the same instructions. I won't tell.

ingredients:
6-8 potatoes or sweet potatoes, peeled, chopped, and boiled
4-6 mushrooms, roughly chopped
1 onion, roughly chopped
6-10 strips of bacon (or ham, reindeer sausage, or kielbasa), cooked and chopped
2/3 cup heavy cream
2/3 cup milk
1 cup cheddar cheese, shredded
1T butter
2T flour
1T chives
1T parsley
salt and pepper to taste

1 Melt the butter or oil in a small saucepan and sauté the onions and mushrooms on low until they are tender and just starting to caramelize.

2 While they're cooking, dump the boiled and chopped potatoes into a large baking dish, and scatter the chopped bacon over them. This is also a good time to preheat your oven to 350 degrees.

3 As soon as the onions and mushrooms are cooked, turn off the heat and stir in the flour until the veggies are evenly covered. Stir in the cream, then turn the heat back on to medium-low.

4 The sauce will start to thicken quickly, so keep stirring and slowly add in the milk. Add salt and pepper to taste. The sauce should thicken to the consistency of runny gravy, add more milk if needed.

5 Pour the sauce over the potatoes and bacon. Cover all with the shredded cheddar and sprinkle the chives and parsley on top. Bake for 20 minutes.

thai chicken & sweet potato noodle bowls

BY MĒGAN ANCHETA

serves 3-4

Thai Sweet Potato Noodle Bowls are packed with fresh veggies and tender chicken. A spicy almond satay sauce adds a serious amount of Thai-style flavor!

Ingredients for the sauce:
1 1/2 tablespoons sesame oil
1 1/2 tablespoons Mae Ploy Yellow Curry Paste
2 garlic cloves, minced
1 teaspoon fresh grated ginger
1/2 cup canned coconut milk (full fat)
1/4 cup water
3 tablespoons almond butter
2 teaspoons fresh squeezed lime juice
2 teaspoons Red Boat Fish Sauce

Ingredients for the noodles:
1 1/2 tablespoons sesame oil
2 large sweet potatoes, spiralized (about 10 cups total)
1 large red bell pepper, thinly sliced in 1-inch pieces
1/4 cup water
6 oz. baby spinach
2 cups diced cooked chicken (I use rotisserie)

Ingredients for the garnish:
lime wedges
chopped cashews
cilantro
green onion

Make the sauce:

1 Warm 1 1/2 tablespoons sesame oil in a small skillet over medium-high heat. Add the Mae Ploy Yellow Curry Paste, garlic, and ginger. Stir continuously and fry until fragrant, about 2-3 minutes.

2 Add the coconut milk, water, almond butter, lime juice, and Red Boat Fish Sauce. Whisk until smooth. Remove from heat.

Make the noodles:

3 Warm 1 1/2 tablespoons sesame oil in a 12-inch skillet (I used my favorite 12-inch cast iron skillet) over medium-high heat. Add the sweet potato noodles and red bell pepper and sauté for 5 minutes.

4 Add the water to the pan, cover, and cook for another 2 minutes (do not remove the lid during this time, you are steaming the noodles).

5 Remove the lid (you won't need it again), and carefully add the baby spinach (you may need to add half, then stir, then add the remaining half to prevent spillage).

6 When the baby spinach is mostly wilted, add the diced cooked chicken, and the sauce. Carefully toss all of the ingredients together. When everything is just combined, remove from heat and serve.

7 Garnish with lime wedges and chopped cashews.

those who do not shrink back

She ran up to the window on full alert, stalking some prey she saw outside. And maybe it was a bird, or a rabbit, or a velociraptor, but I don't think so. It was windy that day and I'm willing to bet it was a leaf.

And, friends, here's the deal: Today, like any day, is likely to put things in our sight that seem like a threat, or a prey, or something to get all worked up over. And it might be real – we might really need to sit up and stalk that thing, ready to take it down at first opportunity.

But it might be a leaf. It might not be a threat at all. All those worries, anxieties, fears, insecurities...they might not be as bad as we think. It might just be the wind. (Or it could be a velociraptor. You never know.)

Every morning dozens of birds are outside these windows, and the cats are captive. They can't get at them but it doesn't stop them from dreaming about it.

We do this, too: We watch, captive and longing. But what if the glass was removed? Would we go for the dream? Would we take the risk? Or would we make excuses, and pretend the glass was still there?

We are all called to something out of our comfort zone, whether it's adoption, having a large family, homeschooling, starting a business, involvement in a ministry, or anything else. But so often we demur with, "Oh, I could never do that," and put others on a pedestal while we hide from responsibility and leadership.

61

It didn't start with us, though – it's been going on a looong time. My favorite example is in 1 Samuel 10, when Saul has been anointed king. When the announcement comes, he is nowhere to be found.

> So they inquired again of the Lord, "Is there a man still to come?" and the Lord said, "Behold, he has hidden himself among the baggage."
> - 1 Samuel 10:22

Saul had been called into royalty, but he was hiding. HIDING. Can you imagine it? *Behold, the great warrior who will lead your people.* He's *right behind those suitcases, to the left of the hatbox.*

We should never confuse humility with cowardice. It isn't humility to shrink back or to feign being "less than" when God has called us to something. It is cowardice and disobedience.

Sure, waiting for a promise is God's work. So many things are out of our control; there is so much we have to surrender. But there is a lot that we do, too.

The main thing we do is live by faith, not shrinking back, ignoring all of our excuses and fears.

> "Yet a little while,
>   and the coming one will come and will not
>   delay;
> but my righteous one shall live by faith,
>   and if he shrinks back,
> my soul has no pleasure in him."
>
> But we are not of those who shrink back and are destroyed, but of those who have faith and preserve their souls.
>
> - Hebrews 10:37-39

We should not confuse resting and waiting with shrinking back. We're not resting and waiting if we're just too afraid to step forward and put ourselves out there when God has called us to go. We have to let go of our fears of failing, our fears of being seen, our fears of people noticing our efforts and imperfections. We have to stop seeing every stray threat as a velociraptor, and recognize that they are mostly just leaves.

God knows we need to hear Him in these steps, and He wants to be heard. We tend to feel so much pressure to figure things out on our own, though. We want to get everything right the first time, and we know how unlikely that is. So why is He calling us to something that is going to expose us and reveal our imperfections?

He wants us to lean in and know our need for Him. He wants us to trust Him. And He wants us to worship Him and nothing else – not our fears, not our successes. Perfectionism reveals those forms of idolatry.

Have you ever looked at a copy of the Declaration of Independence? Did you ever notice that none of the signatures at the bottom are perfectly lined up? Hancock's signature is huge in the middle, and others are sort of lined up in rows. But it is obvious that no one was standing over the men as they signed and pledged their sacred honor, saying, "No, that's off center, it's going to look funny. We'll have to redo it and start over."

No one micromanaged the signatures. They meticulously worked the words of the document over and over, but the signatures, like the lives they represent, were real, imperfect, and genuine. They had bigger things to worry about than perfection; they had a destiny to lead their nation and change the world.

Just like us.

We cannot move forward if we worship our fears more than we worship our Father. God will not bring fulfillment to our promise if we refuse to be found when He calls us. But He has so much grace for us as we draw near to Him in our need.

He knows we can't figure everything out on our own, and He doesn't want us to, anyway. Learning to hear God includes learning to discern between what we think we're supposed to be doing (which is self-imposed pressure) and what God is really asking of us (which is obedience and surrender and trust). If the answers were always easy and obvious, we'd take credit for far too much. We wouldn't need Him; we'd be our own idol. And that would lead to a host of other problems, many of which we'd be willfully blind to at that point.

He loves us too much not to press us toward Him.

So if you are in that place of pressing and calling right now, be encouraged:

This opportunity to step out is the sweet spot of His protection, leading you to the maturity that moves you forward.

...[be] strengthened with all
power, according to His glorious
might, for all *endurance*
and *patience* with *joy* ;
giving thanks to the Father, who
has qualified you to share in the
inheritance of the saints in light.

- colossians 1:11-12

study guide

This flexible, light-yoked guide is for you to use on your own or with a small group. We've included questions to use for personal journaling or group discussion, scripture to study, copy down, and memorize, and short prompts for prayer. It's not homework or another thing to add to your list – it's just movement forward and rest for your soul, friends.

grace to it

questions

What am I doing in this season that represents God's word in action?

What is God calling me toward that I feel unqualified in?

How can I trust God more in this situation?

scripture

Zechariah 4, Haggai 2

prayer

Lord, You are stretching and growing my capabilities as I trust You. Help me to represent You well! Thank You for trusting me with this work and letting me partner with You in it.

telling our feelings where to go

questions

What concerns have been weighing on me lately?

What would it take for them to feel lifted away? What would that feel like?

What specific requests do I need to pray for right now?

scripture

1 Thessalonians 5:16-18, 1 Peter 5:6-7

prayer

Jesus, thank You for caring about everything that is weighing on me. Right now, I need [insert specific requests]. I know You know my needs, but You want to hear me ask You and trust You with them. Please help me also to be discerning of my thoughts and feelings, and to filter them through Your truth.

falling forward

questions

What are some examples of people around me doing brave things?

What are my most common excuses for not taking the next brave step?

How does God answer me when I surrender those excuses to Him?

scripture

Matthew 14:22-33

prayer

Jesus, thank You for Your example and the example of others around me who are doing brave things. Help me to hear You clearly and not make excuses when You tell me to step out.

made for greatness

questions

How have I seen God provide, heal, restore, transform, ease the burden, or make a way for me in the past?

In what situations do I need God to do those things right now? What might that look like?

Who is watching as I take my next steps forward? What is my brave obedience showing them about God?

scripture

Genesis 12:1-9, Exodus 14:21-31, Joshua 4:23-24

prayer

God, You do mighty things for Your people! You haven't stopped doing them. Help me to trust You for those mighty things so I can move where You're calling me.

the journey to high places

questions

Where have I been pulling myself up by my bootstraps when worship, prayer, and surrender would move me forward faster?

Where is Jesus is calling me to that feels like an impossible height?

What areas in my life are surrendered to fear instead of to Him?

scripture

Habakkuk 3:17-19

prayer

Jesus, I am going to worship You instead of my fears and excuses. Thank You for understanding my concerns and knowing my heart. Help me to run to You in worship, prayer, and surrender when I am tempted to give in to fear.

when our favor looks like fear

questions

What current obstacle is in front of you?

What is your biggest fear about moving forward?

What might it look like if that threat turned out to be your greatest favor, or what you've longed for?

scripture

Psalm 27

prayer

Holy Spirit, thank You for speaking to me and giving me answers even before I realize it. Help me to see past the enemy's threats to the victory and triumph You want for me. Thank You for the honor of leading others toward victory as I walk in brave obedience.

facing the future without fear

questions

What next step do I sense God leading me toward today?

What fears seem to be blocking me from taking that step?

As I touch each of those fears, handing them to Jesus in prayer, what do I sense Him saying to me in love? Can I sit with Jesus and allow His love to cast out that fear?

scripture

Romans 8:1, 1 John 4:18

prayer

Father, thank You for knowing my frame and going with me, ahead of me, and behind me. Remind me of Your presence as I take a risk. Show me Your hand and help me to lean on You as I move forward. I want to live a life that is pleasing to You and one that deepens my connection to You and helps me to grow to be more like You.

good for you

questions

Where have I struggled with thinking less of myself because of my mistakes? What does God say about that?

What good things have I thought less of because of a bad experience? What does God say about those things?

How is God growing me in the things I am overcoming in this season?

scripture

1 Peter 2:1-10, James 1:17

prayer

God, thank You for everything! Every good thing comes from You. You protect me in the things that aren't good. You help me overcome hard situations and bad experiences. Help me to walk in forgiveness and wholeness, knowing You are the redeemer who makes all things new.

lessons from my garden

questions

In what areas or situations am I hanging on to control, concerning myself with the outcome?

How can I let those areas and situations become fertile soil for deepening my trust in the Lord?

What steps will I take to submit those areas to the Lord?

scripture

Philippians 1:3-11

prayer

Father, I give up control to You, acknowledging that You are caring for everything seen and unseen. I praise You for working out a master plan, and You will take every good work You've begun and bring it to completion for Your glory. Show me my next step, and help me to walk bravely, knowing You are with me and equipping me and covering all with grace.

in the upheaval

questions

What have I done before that has prepared me for this next step?

If God answered all my prayers, would I be satisfied with what I asked for? Or would I feel like I'd left some things out and settled for less?

What else do I need to ask God for?

scripture

Psalm 20, 1 John 5:1-5

prayer

God, thank You for always answering me. You are always doing more than I am aware of, and growing my tent pegs farther than I realize. Help me to adjust quickly to new routines and be patient with myself in the growing process.

those who do not shrink back

questions

What does living by faith look like for me right now?

Do I struggle with fears of failing, fears of being seen, or fears of people noticing my efforts and imperfections? What would help me surrender these to Jesus?

How is God pressing me close to Him right now, and developing maturity in me?

scripture

Hebrews 10:14-31

prayer

God, You know all my ways and desires. Help me to walk in faith, trusting You and having grace for myself as I follow You forward.

notes

1. Isaiah 36:14-16a.

2. *Rejoice always, pray without ceasing, give thanks in all circumstances; for this is the will of God in Christ Jesus for you.* (1 Thessalonians 5:16-18)

3. C.S. Lewis, *Mere Christianity* (New York: MacMillan Publishing Company, 1952), 125.

4. Charles Kingsley, *Westward Ho!*, 2 vols. (New York: J.F. Taylor and Company, 1899), 1:24.

5. See Genesis 32:22-32.

6. *There is no fear in love, but perfect love casts out fear. For fear has to do with punishment, and whoever fears has not been perfected in love.* (1 John 4:18)

7. *Behold, I am doing a new thing; now it springs forth, do you not perceive it? I will make a way in the wilderness and rivers in the desert.* (Isaiah 43:19)

8. *Or which one of you, if his son asks him for bread, will give him a stone? Or if he asks for a fish, will give him a serpent? If you then, who are evil, know how to give good gifts to your children, how much more will your Father who is in heaven give good things to those who ask him!* (Matthew 7:9-11)

9. *And we know that for those who love God all things work together for good, for those who are called according to his purpose.* (Romans 8:28)

10. Theodore Roosevelt, "Citizenship in a Republic" (speech, Paris, April 23, 1910), Theodore Roosevelt Center, https://www.theodorerooseveltcenter.org/Learn-About-TR/TR-Encyclopedia/Culture-and-Society/Man-in-the-Arena.aspx.

11. *But my righteous one shall live by faith, and if he shrinks back, my soul has no pleasure in him."* But *we are not of those who shrink back and are destroyed, but of those who have faith and preserve their souls.* (Hebrews 10:38-39)

also by shannon guerra

CAPABLE

STEADFAST

RESILIENT

GROWING

SEEN

ALLIED

the Work That God Sees series
prayerful motherhood in the midst of the overwhelm

Moms, you pour yourselves out every day. How about some powerful refilling, in small, easy doses?

Short chapters. White space. Deep down hope, and out loud laughter. Because you have what it takes. You are watched over and known by the God who notices every detail, and He meets you in these mundane moments and is breathing them into mighty movement.

Work That God Sees is available as six individual little books, or as a complete, all-in-one edition with the content from all six books (including the snarky recipes, crafty patterns, and questions for personal journaling or small group discussion) plus 25 pages of extra stories, recipes, and lessons you can learn at someone else's expense.

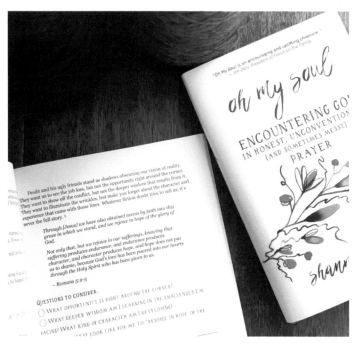

Oh My Soul

encountering God in honest, unconventional (and sometimes messy) prayer

What if there was **one thing** you could do that would always, without fail, make you more **whole** and **healed** and **at peace** than you were the day before...would you do it?

What if, at the same time, that one thing transformed the world around you?

This is what happens when we encounter God, living in His presence, in continual conversation with Him.

We want to hear God better, and to know His will for all the messy, mundane details of our life. But does He still speak to us when we are distracted, grumpy, overwhelmed, and unprepared? How can we have "quiet time" with God when there's no quiet, and no time? Can we really know the will of God and move forward in obedience, in spite of our fears and failures?

And, if we're really honest with Him, will He strike us with lightning? Or will we end up praying with boldness and authenticity like never before?

Available as the original book, companion journal, and 21-day devotional study.

upside down

understanding and supporting attachment in adoptive and foster families

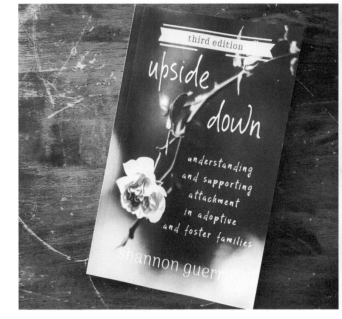

This book gives hope to adoptive and foster families, and the lowdown for those who love them.

Adoptive and foster families working through attachment issues often feel alone, but their communities can intentionally be part of the solution instead of unintentionally being part of the problem. Without that support, adoptive and foster families live in isolation.

Shannon Guerra learned this firsthand after she and her husband adopted two of their children in 2012. She started writing shockingly transparent blog posts about what her family was going through at home, at the doctor's office, and in her heart as a mama.

And then adoptive and foster families started writing back.

Their overwhelming, unanimous theme was, **"This is what I've wanted to tell people for so long. I wish everyone who knows our family could read this."**

This book is the result. In about 100 pages, *Upside Down* provides information and insight that transforms an outsider's assumptions into an insider's powerful perspective. Because adoptive and foster families should never feel alone, and our communities can be equipped to make sure they never feel that way again.

the ABIDE series

a year of growing deep + wide

volume titles:

rest in the running

hope in the waiting

clarity in the longing

bravery for the next step

obedience to move forward

surrendering to win

ABIDE is off the beaten path: A 6-volume series of fully illustrated books that are part devotional, part coffee table book, part magazine. These six beautiful books will lead you further into the presence of God as you grow deep and wide, pressing forward in these seasons that stretch us. Each book contains full color photographs, a light-yoked study section for personal or small group use, an extra recipe or two, and powerful encouragement that meets you where you're at and moves you forward.

one more thing...

Need a little white space in the chaos?

You are warmly invited to copperlightwood.com, where we're transparent about finding peace in the hard moments and beauty in the mess. I hope you'll hit the subscribe button and poke around all the posts and videos. Just keep in mind that it's a little unpolished here, so watch out for the Legos on the floor.

Bless you, friend,
Shannon Guerra

connect:
gab: shannonguerra
mewe: shannonguerra
telegram: Shannon Guerra
clouthub: shannonguerra
facebook: copperlightwood
instagram: copperlightwood
goodreads: shannonguerra
pinterest: copperlightwood

email:
shannon@copperlightwood.com

CPSIA information can be obtained
at www.ICGtesting.com
Printed in the USA
BVHW022005270721
613015BV00003B/14